FOR CARA JOY, WITH LOVE   —CBW

TO HIP-HOP   —FM

 little bee books

An imprint of Bonnier Publishing USA
251 Park Avenue South, New York, NY 10010
Text copyright © 2019 by Carole Boston Weatherford
Illustrations copyright © 2019 by Frank Morrison
All rights reserved, including the right of reproduction in whole or in part in any form. Little Bee Books is a
trademark of Bonnier Publishing USA, and associated colophon is a trademark of Bonnier Publishing USA.
Manufactured in China   HUH 1018
First Edition 10 9 8 7 6 5 4 3 2 1
Library of Congress Cataloging-in-Publication Data
Names: Weatherford, Carole Boston, 1956– author. | Morrison, Frank, 1971– illustrator. | Title: The roots of
rap: 16 bars on the 4 pillars of hip-hop / by Carole Boston Weatherford; illustrated by Frank Morrison Jr.
Description: First edition. | New York, NY: Little Bee Books, 2019.
Identifiers: LCCN 2018007507 | Subjects: LCSH: Rap (Music)—History and criticism—Juvenile literature.
Classification: LCC ML3531 .W43 2018 | DDC 782.42164909—dc23
LC record available at https://lccn.loc.gov/2018007507
ISBN 978-1-4998-0411-9

littlebeebooks.com
bonnierpublishingusa.com

Dear Readers,

I first encountered hip-hop when I was growing up in the Bronx. This particular style of music gave me energy and freedom, and it helped me focus on what I wanted to do with my life. I started deejaying as a teenager, and thanks to support from my family and friends, my career in music took off soon thereafter.

Hip-hop and rap aren't often featured in children's books, so this offering from Carole Boston Weatherford and Frank Morrison is truly special. It provides a wonderful introduction to both the sounds and the artists who paved the way in this genre, many of whom were, and continue to be, role models to me.

My hope is that you will be encouraged to learn more about rap and its roots, along with all the artists who have shaped and continue to make this genre what it is today.

—Swizz Beatz,
*Rapper, DJ, and
Record Producer*

Folktales, street rhymes, spirituals—rooted in spoken word.

Props to poets Hughes and Dunbar; published. Ain't you heard?

Soul man James Brown shouting, "I'm black and I'm proud."

Giving birth to funk—bass line pulsing loud.

BA BUMP BA BUMP BA BOOM BOOM BUZZ   BA BUMP BA BUMP BA BOOM BOOM BUZZ

The origins go way back—beyond old school.

But it is in the seventies that rappers start to rule.

Crews with cans of paint spray tags on subway trains.

Writers from every borough take risks to make a name.

Graffiti is thrown on buildings, bridges, and billboard signs

all along the Manhattan, Queens, Bronx, and Brooklyn lines.
BA BUMP BA BUMP BA BOOM BOOM SPSSSSSSSSSS BA BUMP BA BUMP BA BOOM BOOM SPSSSS SSSSS

A boom box-toting homey blasts a hot track on a corner.

Passersby four-deep surround a street performer.

With sheets of cardboard for a stage, B-boys bust out moves—

donkey, spider, robot, windmill, rock, lock, spin—to break-dance grooves.

BA BUMP BA BUMP BA BOOM BREAK BREAK BA BUMP BA BUMP BA BOOM BREAK BREAK

Jamaican deejays shouting toasts invent what's now called dub;

remix with twin turntables at soul and reggae clubs.

DJ Kool Herc in the Bronx, block party under his command,

rocks and rocks nonstop; mic clutched in his hand.

BA BUMP BA BUMP BA BOOM CLAP CLAP   BA BUMP BA BUMP BA BOOM CLAP CLAP

Dropping, scratching, beat juggling/matching wax on wheels of steel.

Wordplay, rhyming, triple-timing, keepin' the lyrics real.

Sugarhill Gang, Run-D.M.C., LL Cool J, Kurtis Blow,

Biggie, and the Fat Boys jammin' on the radio.

Nas, Ice Cube, Dr. Dre, Eminem, 50 Cent, Tupac, too.

Grandmaster Flash and the Furious Five; "The Message" ringin' true.

BA BUMP BA BUMP SKA WOP DEE DOO   BA BUMP BA BUMP SKA WOP DEE DOO

Female MCs break it down: Salt-N-Pepa and TLC.

Queen Latifah sports a crown, reigning like royalty.

All around her kingdom, shorties raised on rap

boogie to phat beats in backward baseball caps.

BA BUMP BA BUMP ZOOM ZOOM CLAP CLAP   BA BUMP BA BUMP ZOOM ZOOM CLAP CLAP

A generation voicing stories, hopes, and fears

founds a hip-hop nation. Say holler if you hear.

From Atlanta to Zanzibar, youth spit freestyle freedom sounds.

Hip-hop is a language that's spoken the whole world 'round.

BA BUMP BA BUMP SHA BOOM BOP BUZZ   BA BUMP BA BUMP SHA BOOM BOP BUZZ

AUTHOR'S NOTE

I was not raised on rap, but I was rooted in the African American musical- and spoken-word traditions that preceded it. I heard my grandmothers telling stories and reciting proverbs. On city sidewalks and asphalt playgrounds, I joined in jump rope and hand-clap rhymes. In fourth grade, I memorized poems by Harlem Renaissance writer Langston Hughes. I also listened to James Brown's "Say It Loud—I'm Black and I'm Proud" on the radio, and to my father's collection of jazz records, which included Ella Fitzgerald, an originator of scat.

By the time I was an adolescent and young adult, my musical tastes shifted from soul to rock to disco and finally back to jazz. In my twenties, I attended literary readings featuring Black Arts Movement poets such as Nikki Giovanni, Sonia Sanchez, and Haki R. Madhubuti. I also began writing and performing jazz poetry, sometimes to musical accompaniment. I identified with spoken word tracks like Gil Scott-Heron's "The Revolution Will Not Be Televised" and The Last Poets' "This Is Madness."

Rap was not really on my radar, even though I heard rap on the radio and partied to the infectious beats of the Sugarhill Gang and the Fat Boys.

The emerging medium finally caught my attention when Grandmaster Flash and the Furious Five released "The Message" in 1982. The song's beat and bold social commentary on urban poverty resonated with me. It was then that I realized rap was not some passing fad.

After that, I took notice when women like Queen Latifah, Salt-N-Pepa, and TLC took the mic. But I still did not foresee the rise of hip-hop culture.

By 1999, when *The Miseducation of Lauryn Hill* won the Album of the Year Grammy, rap was becoming the language of global youth culture. Today, hip-hop intersects not only with the arts, but also with politics, commerce, and pop culture.

If I were a young poet today, I might be a rapper. Instead, I am an English professor who teaches a course about hip-hop. I drive home the point that hip-hop is poetry at its most powerful.

Peace and power,

"C.B. Dub"

ILLUSTRATOR'S NOTE

August 11th is not only my birthday, it's also the birth date of hip-hop. On a late summer night in 1973, DJ Kool Herc threw the first hip-hop party in the Boogie Down Bronx. From that day forward, Herc would forever be known as the father of hip-hop. It took 10 more years of developing in the streets of New York before I'd be blown out of my knee-high tube socks by its sounds.

"Party people, can y'all get funky?" from "Planet Rock" by Afrika Bambaataa. "Two years ago, a friend of mine/Asked me to say some MC rhymes," from "Sucker M.C.'s" by Run-D.M.C. I was 11 years old in the backyard of my grandmother's house listening to my one-speaker radio when I first heard these groundbreaking hits. I was hooked!

I had no idea on that hot summer afternoon in 1983 that these cool, new sounds would become the music of my generation. Rap's beats and lyrics had busted through ceilings and knocked down doors to establish its place in America's musical landscape. Its pioneers were the first wave of urban restorers, as hip-hop repurposed light poles, cardboard boxes, radios, sneakers, clothes, spray paint, turntables, and yes, records, to create a cultural atmosphere to exist in. The music sampled bits and pieces from the music of previous generations, connecting a bridge between the past and present, and paying homage to its roots.

I'm older now and hip-hop culture isn't as apparently present in my life as it was back in my youth. It's even deeper now, it's in my DNA. You will undoubtedly see it in this book. My fine art will certainly contain a tag or ten. I'm wearing my shell toes now as I write this and my 1980's playlist is currently bumping "My Philosophy" by KRS-One over the speakers.

What I admire about this culture is the diversity, the ingenuity, the sheer tenacity to rock forward regardless of what is in front of it. The hip-hop generation never listened to "can't" and to this day, refuses to take no for an answer. We battle for greatness on the block, the streets, and in the neighborhood and city to achieve the same results as an Olympian: to be the best in the world. I will end this with a rap that my brother Ben wrote that I memorized:

"It was prophesied way back in time

that hip-hop would evolve and blow your mind.

It would come take over the earth

blow away generations with just one verse."

Peace,

B-boy—a break-dancer (see *break dancing*)

beats—the rhythm line for a rap song

boogie—to dance

boom box—a portable cassette or CD player with two or more loudspeakers and a carrying handle

break dancing—a style of street dance that originated among African American and Puerto Rican youth in New York City during the late 1980s; also known as B-boying

DJ—a person who mixes and scratches beats with records on turntables

dub—a musical genre pioneered by reggae artists in the late 1960s and distinguished by instrumental remixes and strong drum and bass lines

folktale—a story originating from the oral tradition of a culture

freestyle—a style of rap in which the lyrics are improvised or created on the spot without rehearsal

funk—a danceable form of music conceived by African American musicians in the 1960s; it grew out of soul music, rhythm and blues, and jazz, and emphasized electric bass and drums to create a strong rhythmic groove

graffiti—a street art genre consisting of writings or drawings that are illegally spray-painted, scribbled, or scratched onto vehicles, walls, bridges, or other property

hip-hop—a form of youth expression that originated in New York City in the late 1970s and included four pillars: graffiti, break dancing, rapping/MCing, and DJing/scratching/turntablism

homey—short for homeboy or homegirl, meaning someone from home

jam—when two or more musicians make music in an informal setting

MC—a writer/performer of rap lyrics

phat—excellent, gratifying, or very attractive

props—respect or credit

rap—spoken or chanted rhyming lyrics that are performed to a beat; its components are content, flow, and delivery

remix—an audio or video clip that has been altered by adding, removing, or changing parts of the original recording

scratching—manipulating sounds with one's hands in order to create and mix music with vinyl records, turntables, and a DJ mixer

shorty—child; also spelled "shawty"

spirituals—religious folk songs that originated with enslaved African Americans

spit—to perform rap lyrics

street rhymes—playground, jump rope, or handclapping chants passed down from generation to generation of children

toast—a rhythmic, rhyming story spoken aloud about heroic characters and events; a form of African American folk poetry

turntable—a device for playing vinyl sound recordings; part of a record player, the turntable has an arm with a stylus (needle) that vibrates between the grooves of a record to produce sound

vinyl—a disc-shaped sound recording that is played on a turntable

HIP-HOP WHO'S WHO

Biggie Smalls, also known as the Notorious B.I.G. (1972–1997)—stage names of Christopher George Latore Wallace, a rapper from Brooklyn, New York

Kurtis Blow (1959–)—stage name of Kurtis Walker, a rapper, singer, songwriter, record producer, DJ, and minister. He was the first commercially successful rapper and the first to sign with a major record label.

James Brown (1933–2006)—a rhythm and blues singer known as the Godfather of Soul and the Hardest-Working Man in Show Business

Dr. Dre (1965–)—stage name of Andre Romelle Young, a record producer, rapper, and entrepreneur who co-founded Death Row Records and co-founded Beats Electronics, manufacturer of audio products

Paul Laurence Dunbar (1872–1906)—the first African American poet to achieve national acclaim for his publications. Sometimes referred to as the Grandfather of Rap, Dunbar wrote formal verse, but his dialect poems were more popular.

Eminem (1972–)—stage name of Marshall Mathers, a rapper, record producer, and songwriter from Detroit, Michigan

The Fat Boys—a hip-hop trio that emerged from Brooklyn, New York, in the 1980s; its members were Mark Morales ("Prince Markie Dee"), Damon Wimbley ("Kool Rock-Ski"), and Darren Robinson ("Buffy" or "the Human Beatbox")

50 Cent (1975–)—stage name of Curtis James Jackson, a rapper, actor, investor, and entrepreneur from Queens, New York

Grandmaster Flash and the Furious Five—a hip-hop group from the South Bronx in New York City. Formed in 1978, they were a significant force in the early development of hip-hop whose 1982 hit, "The Message," is considered one of the genre's defining songs.

DJ Kool Herc (1955–)—stage name of Clive Campbell, a DJ credited with helping originate hip-hop music in the early 1970s in the Bronx, New York. He is known as the Founder of Hip-Hop and the Father of Hip-Hop.

Ice Cube (1969–)—stage name for O'Shea Jackson Sr., an actor, rapper, songwriter, record producer, screenwriter, and entrepreneur. He is one of the founding artists of what became known as gangsta rap.

Langston Hughes (1902–1967)—a writer whose plainspoken poems and stories about the black experience were first published during the Harlem Renaissance of the 1920s

LL Cool J (1968–)—stage name of James Todd Smith, a rapper, actor, author, and entrepreneur from Bay Shore, New York

Nas (1973–)—stage name for Nasir Bin Olu Jones, a hip-hop recording artist, rapper, record producer, actor, and entrepreneur. He has released eight consecutive platinum and multiplatinum albums and has sold over 25 million records worldwide.

Queen Latifah (1970–)—stage name of Dana Owens, a rapper, singer/songwriter, actress, model, television producer, record producer, and talk show host. She's considered one of hip-hop's pioneer feminists.

Run-D.M.C.—an influential hip-hop group from Queens, New York, founded in 1981 by Joseph Simmons ("Run"), Darryl McDaniels ("D.M.C."), and Jason Mizell ("Jam Master Jay"). They were the first hip-hop group to have a gold album and win a Grammy Award.

Salt-N-Pepa—a hip-hop trio from Queens, New York. Formed in 1985, the group, consisting of Cheryl James ("Salt"), Sandra Denton ("Pepa"), and Pamela Latoya Greene, who would be replaced by Deidre Roper ("DJ Spinderella"), was one of the first all-female rap groups.

The Sugarhill Gang—a hip-hop group whose 1979 hit, "Rapper's Delight," was the first rap single to become a Top 40 hit on the Billboard Hot 100

Tupac Shakur (1971–1996)—known by the stage names 2Pac and briefly Makaveli, Shakur was a rapper, songwriter, and actor who has sold more than 75 million records and is one of the best-selling music artists in history

TLC—a girl group who recorded rhythm and blues, hip-hop, soul, funk, and new jack swing. Comprised of Tionne Watkins ("T-Boz"), Lisa Lopes ("Left Eye"), and Rozonda Thomas ("Chilli"), the group was popular in the 1990s and early 2000s.